GIRLS OF NOBODY

A Memoir of Survival, Silence, and Strength

Sophia J Berg

Copyright © 2025 by Sophia J. Berg

All Rights Reserved.

No portion of this publication may be copied, stored, or shared in any form whether electronic, mechanical, digital, or otherwise without express written permission from the publisher, except in the case of brief quotations used for reviews, articles, or educational citation.

This content is provided for personal use only. Any unauthorized duplication, distribution, or commercial use is strictly prohibited and constitutes a violation of copyright law.

Dedication

To every girl who was ever told she was nobody.

To every survivor who carries invisible scars, yet still finds the courage to rise each day.

To those who never got the chance to tell their stories—this book carries your voices too.

And to the child I once was: you were never nobody. You were always worthy.

Preface

When I first began writing what would eventually become Girls of Nobody, I didn't imagine it would grow into something this large, this heavy, and this necessary. At first, I was simply writing to make sense of my own pain—scribbling down memories in the middle of sleepless nights, trying to release what my mind carried for too long. Those pages were not intended for the world. They were for me, a private act of survival.

But survival is not the same as healing. Healing demanded something more: honesty, courage, and the willingness to risk being seen. For years, I was silent. Silence was safe. Silence was how I protected myself from judgment, disbelief, and shame. Yet silence also protected the very forces that hurt me, allowing them to continue unseen and unchecked.

Slowly, I realized that my story was not just mine. It was the story of countless others whose voices had been stolen. It was the story of a society that often chooses to look away rather than confront the uncomfortable truth of abuse. It was the story of resilience—of what it means to fight not only for justice in the courtroom, but for peace in one's own heart.

This book is not perfect, because healing is not perfect. There are jagged edges in these chapters, memories that still sting, truths that still feel raw. But I believe in their necessity. I believe in naming what was once hidden. And I believe that even the most painful stories can become seeds of change.

As you read, I ask that you carry these pages gently. They are written with vulnerability, not for pity but for understanding. My hope is that Girls of Nobody will not only give voice to survivors, but also ignite empathy in those who may have never walked this path. Abuse thrives in the dark, but when we bring light to it, we strip it of its power.

To the reader holding this book: thank you. Thank you for choosing to listen, to witness, to care. Whether you are a survivor, an ally, or simply someone willing to learn, your presence here matters. And perhaps, together, we can create a world where no girl ever has to feel like "nobody" again.

[Author's Name]

TABLE OF CONTENTS

Introduction 7
Part 1   Innocence Interrupted 10
Chapter 1 – A Childhood Unraveled 12
Chapter 2 – Whispers in the Dark 14
Chapter 3 – The First Betrayal 17
Chapter 4 – Groomed for Silence 21
PART 2 – Captive in Plain Sight 24
Chapter 5 – A World Behind Closed Doors 27
Chapter 6 – The Weight of Secrets 30
Chapter 7 – Shattered Trust 33
Chapter 8 – Silent Cries 37
Chapter 9 – Promises and Predators 40
Chapter 10 – Living in the Shadows 43
PART 3 – The Courage to Speak 46
Chapter 11 – Finding My Voice 49
Chapter 12– When No One Believed Me 51
Chapter 13 – The Power of Telling the Truth
.... 54
PART 4 – Justice and Resistance 57
Chapter 14 – Into the Courts 60
Chapter 15– The Shield of Power 63

Chapter 16 – Small Victories, Heavy Losses . 65

Chapter 17 – Standing Against Giants 68

Part V – Becoming Whole Again 71

Chapter 18 – Healing the Invisible Wounds 73

Chapter 19 – Sisters of Survival 76

Chapter 20 – From Silence to Advocacy 79

Chapter 21 – A Future Beyond "Nobody" 81

Epilogue – The Echo of Survival 84

Acknowledgments 86

Note to the Reader 88

Introduction

There are stories that demand to be told, even when every part of the storyteller trembles at the thought of speaking. They are not the polished tales we share at celebrations, nor the gentle memories that bring smiles in old age. They are raw, unsettling, and, for far too long, buried under silence. Girls of Nobody is born out of that silence the silence of children whose voices were stolen, of young women whose dignity was crushed, of survivors whose scars were dismissed as invisible.

This book is not about fame, wealth, or glory. It is about those who were made to feel like they were nobody the girls who were used, silenced, and forgotten, yet whose lives bear witness to truths the world often chooses not to see. The phrase "girls of nobody" is not a definition but a wound. It reflects how society too often labels survivors of abuse: invisible, unwanted, voiceless. Yet, as these pages will reveal, no girl is truly nobody. Each life carries worth, dignity, and unbreakable spirit, even when the world has tried to strip it away.

The journey that unfolds here is not a straight path from darkness to light. Healing rarely is. Instead, it is an honest exploration of what it means to grow up marked by abuse, to wrestle with betrayal, to stumble under the weight of shame that never belonged to you in the first place. It is about the hollow moments when you feel unseen, and the fire that flickers sometimes faintly, sometimes fiercely that pushes you to rise anyway.

This is not just a personal story. It is also a mirror held up to a larger world where abuse hides behind closed doors, behind wealth and power, and even behind the masks of trusted faces. It is a reminder that exploitation does not always look like the stranger in the alleyway; sometimes it wears a smile, sometimes it offers gifts, sometimes it whispers promises that end in chains.

As you turn these pages, you will meet not only my story but the echo of countless others. For every girl who speaks, there are hundreds more who cannot. Their silence is not consent; it is survival. Their absence from the narrative is not because their pain was less, but because the world made it harder for them to be heard. This book carries their shadows alongside my own voice, because no survivor's story exists in isolation.

But Girls of Nobody is not only about what was taken it is also about what remains. Courage. Resilience. The stubborn belief that life can be reclaimed. It is about learning to see yourself not as broken, but as remade. It is about discovering that being a survivor is not the end of your identity, but the beginning of a new one.

Writing these words has not been easy. At times, I wanted to stop. The memories pressed too hard, the emotions too heavy. But I kept writing because I know that silence is where abusers thrive, and breaking silence is how survivors begin to heal. I write because somewhere, a young girl is wondering if she is the only one. I write because somewhere, a grown woman still carries the secret of her childhood. I write because the truth however painful has the power to set us free.

To every reader, I offer this: read with compassion. The pages that follow are heavy with pain, but they are also laced with hope. If you are a survivor, may you find strength in knowing you are not alone. If you are an ally, may you be moved to listen more deeply and act more boldly. And if you are someone who has never thought much about these hidden stories, may this book open your eyes to a world you cannot ignore.

We are the girls the world tried to make into nobodies. Yet here we are, speaking, writing, refusing to disappear. Our existence is our resistance. Our stories are our power. And through them, we reclaim what was always ours: our voices, our dignity, and our place in the world.

This is Girls of Nobody. Welcome to the journey.

PART 1 INNOCENCE INTERRUPTED

Childhood is meant to be a sanctuary. A time when the world feels wide, yet safe; when dreams stretch beyond the horizon, untouched by cruelty. For most children, innocence is the currency of those years a tender gift, freely carried, gently nurtured. But for some of us, that innocence is not protected. It is stolen. Sometimes slowly, piece by piece. Sometimes violently, in a single moment that fractures life into a "before" and an "after."

I was one of those children.

To the outside world, nothing seemed amiss. I laughed when I was supposed to laugh. I played when I was expected to play. I wore the mask of an ordinary child. But behind closed doors, a different story unfolded. A story of betrayal, confusion, and fear so heavy it wrapped itself around me like a shadow I could not escape. The people who should have guarded my innocence instead became the reason it shattered.

The cruelty of abuse lies not only in what is done to the body, but in what it does to the mind. It teaches you to question your worth before you even understand what worth is. It replaces the natural curiosity of childhood with a constant scanning of danger. It takes the safe rhythm of laughter and interrupts it with silence, shame, and secrets. Innocence is interrupted not just once, but again and again, until you can no longer remember what it felt like to be whole.

For many years, I thought I was alone in this experience. I thought my pain was an anomaly, something so rare it had to be hidden. But as I grew older, I learned an unbearable truth: there are countless others. Girls and boys who carry wounds invisible to the world. Survivors who learned too early how dangerous trust can be. We are scattered across different countries, different cultures, different families, but our stories carry the same echoes.

This part of the book is for that child the one who never had the chance to remain a child. It is for the little girl sitting silently in the corner, too afraid to speak of what happened. It is for the boy who tries to erase his tears before anyone notices. It is for the children who had their innocence interrupted by the cruelty of others, and who carry the consequences long into adulthood.

Here, I will tell the story of how my own innocence was interrupted. Not to sensationalize pain, but to name it honestly. Because abuse thrives in secrecy, and silence feeds shame. By speaking, I begin to reclaim not only my story but the power that was stolen from me.

As you enter these chapters, prepare yourself for the weight of truth. Some of it will be difficult to read. Some of it may stir memories of your own. But alongside the pain, there is also resilience. Alongside the shadows, there are flickers of light. Because even though innocence was interrupted, life did not end there. A new story began one of survival, strength, and, eventually, healing.

This is where it starts. With the child I once was. With the innocence that was taken. With the silence that followed. And with the courage, now, to finally speak.

Chapter 1 – A Childhood Unraveled

Every childhood begins with threads moments of laughter, the warmth of family, the wonder of discovery. For some, those threads weave into a tapestry of safety and belonging. For others, the fabric frays too soon, tugged apart by betrayal until it no longer resembles the innocence it once held. My childhood, though outwardly ordinary, was unraveling long before anyone noticed.

I remember small details more vividly than the larger picture. The smell of the room where secrets lived. The creak of a door opening when I wished it would stay closed. The way my heart would race, even as my face was forced to remain still. These fragments live inside me like broken glass sharp, scattered, impossible to sweep away completely. They are the pieces of a childhood that was never allowed to stay whole.

From the outside, my world looked unremarkable. A child going to school, playing with friends, pretending to dream big. Adults smiled, neighbors waved, teachers asked how I was doing, and I answered in the way children are trained to answer: "I'm fine." But beneath the surface, my life was split in two the visible and the hidden. The visible was ordinary; the hidden was suffocating. Abuse doesn't always roar. Sometimes it whispers, quietly reshaping your understanding of love, trust, and safety until you no longer know what those words mean.

Children aren't born knowing how to keep secrets. They learn. They are taught through fear, through manipulation, through the cold realization that the truth may not protect them. I learned early that my silence was expected. That my words, if spoken, might be twisted or dismissed. So I built a fortress inside myself, brick by brick, hiding what I could not understand, convincing myself that perhaps this was normal. Perhaps this was what love looked like. Perhaps the fault was mine.

Looking back, I see how the unraveling began not in one sudden moment but in many subtle ones. It was the first time I flinched at a touch that should have been safe. It was the way laughter in my home sometimes felt like a mask covering something darker. It was the slow erosion of trust in the very people meant to protect me. Childhood is supposed to be a time of discovery, but for me, discovery meant realizing too soon that the world was not safe.

No child should ever have to carry such knowledge. It is too heavy, too cruel. Yet I carried it quietly, like a stone in my chest. It shaped the way I walked through the world. It shaped the way I looked at myself. Abuse is not only what is done to you. It is what it convinces you to believe about yourself. And I believed I was powerless. I believed I was invisible. I believed, most tragically of all, that I was nobody.

This chapter is not easy to write, and I know it may not be easy to read. But it is necessary. Because silence allows the unraveling to continue unchecked not only in my life, but in the lives of countless others. By telling my story, I honor the child I once was, and I stand in solidarity with every other child who has had their innocence stolen.

Childhood is fragile. It can unravel quietly, thread by thread, without anyone noticing until it is almost gone. Mine did. But here, in these words, I begin the work of weaving those threads into something new not the tapestry that was stolen, but one I claim for myself. One made of truth, resilience, and the belief that even broken childhoods can give rise to unbreakable strength.

Chapter 2 – Whispers in the Dark

Night has a way of magnifying everything the creak of a floorboard, the rustle of curtains, the weight of silence pressing against the walls. For most children, darkness is a space for dreams, a gentle pause between one day and the next. But for me, the night carried whispers. They were not always spoken aloud, yet I heard them as clearly as any voice. They were the whispers of fear, of secrets, of things I could never say but always felt.

It was in the dark that my world shifted most. By day, I could pretend. I could play the role of a smiling child, even if inside I was unraveling. But the night stripped away that mask. In the quiet, there was no distraction, no noise to drown out the memories. I lay awake, listening for footsteps I dreaded, holding my breath at the sound of a door opening, praying for safety that never came.

The whispers were not always external they lived inside me too. They told me to stay silent. They told me no one would believe me. They told me I was at fault. They told me I was weak. Abuse has a way of planting its lies deep in a child's mind until those lies sound like truth. And in the dark, those lies grew louder.

I tried to make sense of what was happening, but children are not equipped with the language of trauma. All I had were feelings shame, confusion, fear and no words big enough to hold them. So I whispered to myself instead. Little prayers, little bargains, little promises: If I can just make it through tonight... If I can stay very still, maybe it won't happen... If I don't speak, maybe it will stop. Those were my whispered survival strategies, repeated night after night, as if silence could somehow shield me.

The cruelest part of darkness is how it isolates. Even in a house full of people, I felt utterly alone. Surrounded by walls, by family, by the hum of ordinary life and yet, when it mattered, no one saw, no one knew. Or perhaps they chose not to. I often wondered if the whispers traveled further than I realized if others heard them too but turned away. That thought made the loneliness sharper, the silence deeper.

And yet, within those whispers, there was also a strange defiance. A voice faint but persistent that said: This is wrong. I did not have the courage to act on it yet, but its presence mattered. It reminded me that even though my innocence was stolen, my spirit was not completely broken. Somewhere deep inside, I still knew the truth. That small whisper would later become a voice, and that voice would eventually become a roar. But in those nights, it was just a flicker fragile, uncertain, but alive.

"Whispers in the Dark" became the story of my childhood nights, but it is also the story of many others. Survivors rarely begin with shouts. Most begin with whispers. Silent screams lodged in the throat, unspoken words that weigh like stones in the chest. We whisper to ourselves because it feels safer than shouting into a world that may not listen. We whisper because secrets, once spoken, can never be undone. We whisper because whispers are the only language we believe we have left.

Now, as I write these words, I think of that little girl who lay awake in the dark, whispering prayers into the silence. She believed she was nobody, but here she is, speaking at last. Her whispers have become witnesses. Her silence has become story. And in telling it, she proves that even the quietest voice, once freed, can carry further than she ever imagined.

Chapter 3 – The First Betrayal

Every story of survival has a beginning, and mine begins with betrayal. Not the betrayal of strangers, not the sudden violence of a world outside, but the slow and quiet undoing from the very place I was meant to be safest.

People often imagine betrayal as a single dramatic moment a knife in the back, a sudden revelation, a shattering event that splits life cleanly into "before" and "after." But for me, the first betrayal was not loud. It was quiet. It was woven into the small details of everyday life, disguised in gestures that seemed harmless to the outside world. It was subtle enough that even I, as a child, could not name it for what it was. All I knew was that something felt wrong. Deeply wrong.

Trust is the natural language of children. We do not learn to doubt until someone teaches us. As children, we believe the words of adults, we lean into their arms, we accept their care as truth. And yet, it is that very trust which becomes the weapon in the hands of those who exploit it. My trust was turned against me, used not to protect but to harm, and in that moment of realization, my childhood began to unravel more swiftly than ever before.

The first betrayal came from someone who should have been a guardian, a protector, a figure of love and safety. Instead, they crossed the line between care and violation, leaving me confused, frightened, and ashamed. I will not offer names here, not because they do not matter, but because betrayal is larger than a single person. It is a pattern, a truth that repeats in the lives of countless children. My betrayal is mine, but it also echoes in the lives of many others.

I remember the day clearly not the exact date, but the feeling. The way the air shifted, the way my body froze though my mind screamed for movement. A touch that lingered too long, a gaze that felt different, a boundary crossed that could never be uncrossed. It was not just the act itself, but the knowledge it carried: the realization that I was no longer safe. That the person I depended on had chosen to harm me. That the world was not what I thought it was.

That was the first betrayal.

And it cut deeper than I could ever describe.

In that moment, I learned something children should never have to learn that the very hands meant to shield me could become the same hands that hurt me. That love and danger could wear the same face. That I could no longer trust the ground beneath me to hold.

The pain of the first betrayal is not only in the act, but in its aftermath. The questions it plants in your soul. Why me? What did I do wrong? Did I deserve this? As a child, I could not separate the abuser's actions from my own sense of self. I believed the whispers of guilt and shame that followed me like shadows. I believed that if I told, no one would believe me or worse, that they would blame me. Silence became my companion, and silence was heavy.

Looking back, I realize how that first betrayal set the stage for everything that followed. It taught me to hide. It taught me to perform normalcy while carrying a secret that burned inside me. It taught me that love could not be trusted, that safety was an illusion, and that my voice was powerless.

But even as I write this, I want to tell that child the one who felt the weight of betrayal before she even had the words for it that she was not wrong. That it was never her fault. That betrayal is not a reflection of the betrayed, but of the betrayer. She was not weak for staying silent; she was surviving. She was not nobody; she was someone whose worth was being hidden, not erased.

The first betrayal left scars, yes, but it also planted a seed of defiance. A seed that would, in time, grow into strength, into resistance, into voice. It would take years decades, even for that seed to break through the soil of silence. But it was there, quietly waiting, even when I thought I was broken beyond repair.

This chapter is not just about my betrayal. It is about the universal truth that betrayal wounds deeper than almost any other hurt. Because it does not only harm the body or the mind it wounds the soul. It fractures trust, it poisons innocence, it alters the way we see the world. And yet, acknowledging it naming it for what it is is the first step toward reclaiming what was taken.

So here I am, naming it.

This was my first betrayal. The beginning of a story I never asked for, but one I now choose to tell. Because in telling it, I take back what was stolen: the truth of my own voice.

Chapter 4 – Groomed for Silence

Silence does not arrive suddenly. It is shaped, molded, and carefully woven into the life of a child until it feels natural, until it feels safer than speaking. By the time I understood that something was terribly wrong in my world, I had already been groomed not only for exploitation, but for silence.

People often imagine grooming as gifts, sweet words, or slow seduction, but it is far more calculated than that. Grooming is psychological preparation. It is teaching a child how to doubt their own instincts, how to question their reality, how to believe that their voice has no power. It is not only about drawing you in it is about shutting you down.

My silence was not accidental. It was demanded, enforced, and reinforced in ways that were both subtle and terrifying. At first, it came as warnings whispered with a smile: No one will believe you. This is our little secret. If you tell, people will think you're lying. Those words seemed harmless on the surface, but they carried heavy weight. For a child desperate to be loved, desperate not to be rejected, those whispers felt binding.

And then came the threats. Not always direct, but enough to tighten the noose around my voice. If you speak, you'll ruin everything. If you say a word, you'll be taken away. If you tell anyone, you'll be the one who gets punished. To a child, those warnings feel like law. Fear kept me frozen, and shame sealed my lips.

What makes grooming so insidious is how it manipulates the natural trust of children. I was taught to see my silence as loyalty, as proof that I was "special," as evidence of some twisted bond. And yet, beneath that lie was the reality: my silence was what kept the abuser safe, not me. It was the shield that allowed them to continue.

I learned to live two lives. In the daylight, I smiled, studied, and laughed as though nothing was wrong. At night, I carried the heavy secret that crushed me. I became skilled at pretending so skilled, in fact, that sometimes even I wondered if I was imagining it all. That was the most dangerous part of being groomed for silence: it made me doubt myself.

I questioned everything. Maybe it wasn't that bad. Maybe I misunderstood. Maybe it was my fault. These thoughts were not mine they were planted, carefully and repeatedly, until I watered them myself with guilt and fear. Grooming had trained me to keep quiet not only with others, but with myself. I swallowed my own truth, convinced it was poison.

Years later, when I began to speak, people would ask, Why didn't you tell someone sooner? Why didn't you cry out? What they don't understand is that silence becomes survival. It becomes the air you breathe, the skin you live in. Breaking it feels impossible when your whole world has taught you that your voice will bring only more pain. Silence, though heavy, felt safer than sound.

And so I kept quiet. I learned to smile when I wanted to cry. I learned to hold secrets that weighed more than my small shoulders could carry. I learned to adapt, to survive, to bury myself beneath layers of obedience and fear. Grooming didn't just teach me to keep silent about the abuse it taught me to silence myself in all areas of life, to shrink, to disappear, to believe that I was nobody.

But here is the truth I wish someone had told me then: silence protects the abuser, not the abused. Silence allows wounds to fester in the dark. Silence convinces us that we are alone when, in reality, thousands of others are carrying the same burden. Silence is not loyalty, nor safety it is bondage.

Breaking that silence would take me years. It would require courage I didn't yet know I had. But the cracks were forming, even then. Deep inside me, there was still a voice a small one, muffled and trembling but alive. It whispered that the shame was not mine. It whispered that the guilt belonged to the one who hurt me, not the child forced into silence.

This chapter is my defiance against that grooming. It is my proof that silence, once broken, loses its grip. Writing these words is my rebellion. My voice, which was once smothered, now fills these pages.

I was groomed for silence, yes. But I am no longer silent.

PART 2 - CAPTIVE IN PLAIN SIGHT

Captivity does not always come with chains, bars, or locked doors. Sometimes, it comes in the form of a smile, a family gathering, a Sunday service, or a classroom where no one notices the quiet child in the corner. Sometimes, captivity hides in plain sight, so invisible that even those closest to you cannot or will not see.

That was the reality of my life. To the outside world, everything looked ordinary. I was just another child navigating school, play, and home life. My laughter seemed genuine. My achievements seemed natural. No one stopped to look beneath the surface. No one suspected that behind the carefully painted picture of "normal," there was a girl imprisoned by secrets too heavy for her small frame.

This is the cruelty of hidden abuse: it thrives not in isolation, but in plain view. The abuser wears the mask of respectability, and society nods in approval. To outsiders, they are kind, responsible, perhaps even admired. Meanwhile, the victim learns to carry pain silently, terrified that if the truth slipped out, no one would believe it.

I lived in that tension daily. I was both seen and unseen. Present, yet invisible. Surrounded by people, yet profoundly alone. My body went to school, to gatherings, to play with friends, but my soul was trapped behind an invisible wall that no one could or perhaps dared to break through.

What makes captivity in plain sight so devastating is the way it erases your sense of reality. When everyone around you sees something different from what you are experiencing, you begin to question yourself. Maybe it isn't happening. Maybe I'm exaggerating. Maybe I'm the problem. Those lies became my prison bars.

And so, I learned to perform. To laugh at the right jokes. To smile when eyes were watching. To excel in school so no one would ask questions. To play the role of the "good child" because that mask shielded me from suspicion. Performance became my survival. Every day was an act, every moment carefully managed so no one would glimpse the truth of my captivity.

But captivity in plain sight leaves traces, even if faint ones. The nervous glances. The flinches that come when someone moves too suddenly. The silence that lingers when others chatter. The hollow look that sometimes creeps into the eyes of a child who has seen too much. I wonder, even now, how many people noticed those cracks in my mask and chose not to ask. How many adults sensed something was wrong but turned away because the truth was too uncomfortable.

That is another cruelty of hidden captivity: it is often protected by denial. It is easier for the world to believe in happy families and smiling children than to confront the nightmare that may be unfolding behind closed doors. And so, silence is not only enforced by the abuser but also by a society that prefers comfort over truth.

Inside, I longed for someone to see me not the mask, but the real me, the terrified child trapped in plain sight. I wanted someone to notice the way my voice faltered, the way my smile sometimes broke too quickly, the way shadows seemed to follow me even in the daylight. I wanted rescue, even when I was too afraid to ask for it.

But rescue never came.

And so, I remained captive in plain sight. My body was free to move through the world, but my spirit was caged by fear, silence, and shame. My prison was invisible, and yet it was suffocating.

Looking back now, I realize how many children live like that sitting in classrooms, walking in neighborhoods, playing in parks carrying secrets no one wants to hear. They are there, hidden in plain view, their captivity masked by forced smiles and quiet obedience. I was one of them. I was nobody's girl, unseen, unheard, unrescued.

But even in captivity, a part of me resisted. A small part. A stubborn spark that whispered: One day, you will be free. One day, your truth will be heard. That spark, though faint, kept me alive through the long nights and silent days.

This chapter is for that child, and for every child still trapped in plain sight. May they be seen. May they be heard. May their captivity end not in silence, but in freedom.

Chapter 5 – A World Behind Closed Doors

Behind every closed door lies a story that outsiders rarely see. For me, those doors were both literal and symbolic. To the world beyond them, I lived an ordinary life schoolwork neatly done, polite manners displayed, a child who seemed quiet but "well-behaved." But the truth existed in another world, the one hidden behind the closed doors of my home, where innocence was stripped away and silence was demanded.

Behind those doors, reality shifted. Laughter turned brittle, smiles felt forced, and shadows grew thick. The world outside might have assumed safety and warmth, but the air within was heavy, laced with fear and unspoken rules. What happened in that space was not to be shared. Not with friends. Not with teachers. Not with anyone. Behind those doors, my identity was reshaped, molded by fear, shame, and survival.

I learned early that closed doors carried meaning. A door shutting softly might mean secrecy. A door slammed in anger meant danger. A door locked behind me meant entrapment. I memorized those sounds the way other children memorized bedtime stories, and each one told me something about what awaited me inside. My body grew tense at the slightest click of a latch, the faintest creak of a hinge. Doors no longer protected me they trapped me.

The world behind closed doors was a stage where roles were assigned, not chosen. My role was obedience. My script was silence. I was taught to play along, to pretend that nothing unusual was happening, to carry the heavy mask of normalcy when the doors finally opened and the outside world caught a glimpse of us. Behind closed doors, truth was distorted until even I began to question whether my own memories were real.

The strangest part of living in that hidden world was how ordinary everything looked to others. To visitors, the home seemed stable. To neighbors, it looked like any other. Yet once those doors shut, the mask slipped, and the nightmare resumed. It was as though the house had two separate lives: one carefully displayed for the world and another locked away for me alone to endure.

That secret life left scars deeper than the acts themselves. It was not only what was done, but the isolation of knowing it was unseen, unheard, unacknowledged. The outside world moved on, busy with its chatter, its schoolyard games, its family meals, while inside I felt the walls closing in. Behind those doors, time slowed. Each minute stretched endlessly. I was a prisoner of silence, a child navigating storms no one else knew existed.

The weight of living in two worlds one visible, one hidden was crushing. By day, I was the girl who smiled faintly at classmates, who tried to answer correctly when teachers called on me, who did everything possible not to draw attention. By night, I was the girl behind closed doors, terrified of what might happen, rehearsing excuses in my head in case anyone asked about the shadows beneath my eyes.

No one did.

No one asked.

And so, my world remained divided the public face and the private prison. The door was the boundary between them, a fragile barrier that no one dared to open fully.

Looking back, I see now how many children live in similar worlds, their stories hidden just out of sight, behind doors that look ordinary from the outside. We pass those homes every day without knowing the storms raging within. We smile at families without realizing what truths their walls contain. I was one of those children. My world was behind closed doors, but my silence was never proof of safety it was proof of survival.

Writing this now, I fling those doors wide open. I allow the light to pour into the spaces once covered in shadow. Because the truth is, doors cannot hold secrets forever. They may silence a child for a season, but eventually, voices break through. And when they do, the world behind closed doors is revealed for what it truly was: a place of captivity, but also the birthplace of resilience.

This chapter is my way of opening those doors, of showing what was hidden, of refusing to let the walls keep the truth imprisoned any longer.

Chapter 6 – The Weight of Secrets

Secrets have weight. They may be invisible to the eye, but to the soul, they are crushing. When you are a child, carrying even the smallest secret can feel enormous like a backpack filled with stones you are too small to lift. And when the secrets are not small but shattering, they can bury you alive.

I learned the heaviness of secrets far too young. Each day I held inside me what I could not tell. Each night I lay awake with unspoken words pressing against my chest, suffocating me, demanding release but finding no escape. My secret was not just a memory of what had been done to me it was the silence around it, the lies wrapped around it, the unshakable fear that if I spoke, everything would collapse.

Carrying that weight distorted me. Outwardly, I appeared calm, quiet, maybe even "well-behaved." Inwardly, I was drowning. Every smile was a performance, every conversation carefully measured to avoid revealing too much. I became hyperaware of myself, editing every word before it left my lips, terrified that I might accidentally let the truth slip out. Even in moments of joy, the secret lingered, pulling me back down like an anchor.

The strangest part was how the secret felt both too heavy to carry and too dangerous to put down. I wanted to tell someone anyone. I longed for release, for a trusted ear to take even a fraction of the burden from me. But the fear was stronger. Fear of not being believed. Fear of being blamed. Fear of losing the little fragments of stability I clung to. Fear that my voice, once released, would cause more harm than silence ever could.

So, I carried it alone.

The weight of secrets doesn't only rest on the heart; it seeps into the body. My shoulders seemed to droop under the invisible load. My stomach twisted with anxiety. My sleep was broken, haunted by the unspoken. Even my breathing felt shallow, as though my lungs themselves were crushed beneath what I could not share.

Childhood should be a time of lightness, of curiosity, of carefree exploration. But mine was a time of gravity. Of heaviness. Of secrets.

And with every passing day, the secret grew heavier. Because secrets multiply. One silence demands another, and then another, until soon you are not only hiding the truth of what happened but also hiding the truth of who you are. The secret of the abuse became the secret of my sadness, the secret of my shame, the secret of my fear. I was a child hidden inside herself, wrapped in layers of silence so thick that even I sometimes forgot what my voice sounded like.

Yet, in carrying the weight of those secrets, I also carried something else: resilience. It may sound strange, but the very act of surviving that silence taught me endurance. Every day I woke up and carried that burden, I was unknowingly building strength. It was not the kind of strength anyone should have to learn, but it was strength nonetheless the strength to keep breathing, to keep moving, to keep waiting for a moment when I might finally be free.

The tragedy is that children should not be asked to carry such loads. Secrets of abuse, of betrayal, of pain these are not meant for small shoulders. And yet, so many of us do. We carry them into our teens, into our adulthood, until the weight bends our backs, shapes our choices, and shadows our lives. Some of us find ways to set them down. Some of us never do.

I carried my secret for years, and it left marks on me that no one could see. But today, as I write these words, I begin to unburden myself. Each sentence, each confession, is a stone lifted from my chest. The weight does not vanish all at once it lingers, it shifts but it becomes lighter with every truth spoken.

The weight of secrets nearly crushed me. But here, in this book, I lay them down. Not just for myself, but for every child who has ever carried more than they should. You are not alone. Your silence is not your fault. And your secrets, though heavy, do not have to be yours forever.

Chapter 7 – Shattered Trust

Trust is the invisible thread that holds the fabric of childhood together. It is what allows a child to sleep peacefully at night, to reach for an adult's hand without hesitation, to believe in promises spoken aloud. For most children, trust is something instinctive they do not question it, because they have not yet been given a reason to doubt. For me, that thread was torn far too soon, leaving the fabric of my world frayed, unstable, and dangerous.

The first betrayal cracked the foundation. The grooming sealed my silence. The secrets weighed me down. But the moment I truly felt the world collapse was when my trust was shattered. And when trust is broken in a child, it is not only a loss it is an earthquake that reshapes everything that follows.

I could no longer look at adults the same way. The ones who should have protected me had chosen to harm me, and that truth lodged deep in my bones. If the people closest to me could not be trusted, then who could? My teachers, who smiled kindly but never looked closely enough to see my pain? My friends, who laughed with me on playgrounds but would not understand the darkness I carried? Even God, whom I was told to pray to, felt distant and silent in the face of my suffering. Trust had become a luxury I could no longer afford.

The shattering of trust is not always loud. It does not announce itself with a crash or a scream. Sometimes, it breaks quietly, like glass cracking beneath a surface, invisible until the whole pane falls apart. I did not wake up one morning and decide to stop trusting; it eroded slowly, with every silence I was forced to keep, with every lie I was told, with every dismissal of my invisible wounds. The world taught me to expect disappointment, to prepare for betrayal, to guard myself from everyone even those who meant no harm.

And yet, the cruel irony is that children are still dependent, even when trust is gone. I had no choice but to live under the same roof, to eat at the same table, to obey the same voices. My body remained in the custody of people I feared, even while my heart screamed for freedom. That dependence only deepened my distrust. I felt trapped in a cage where the very ones holding the key were also the ones who had built the bars.

Losing trust altered me. It made me cautious where I should have been carefree. It made me silent when I should have spoken. It made me suspicious of kindness, wary of love, skeptical of promises. Even simple things a hand reaching out, a compliment, a smile felt like potential traps. I became a child who flinched at warmth, who withdrew at closeness, who tested every word and gesture against the memory of betrayal.

What people do not always understand is that trust, once shattered in childhood, is not easily rebuilt. It leaves a scar on the soul. Later, as an adult, even in safe spaces, even with good people, a part of me still braced for the rug to be pulled from under me. A voice inside whispered: Don't get too comfortable. Don't believe too quickly. Don't let your guard down. Remember what happened the last time you trusted.

But I also want to honor the truth here: that broken trust, though devastating, is not the end of the story. It wounded me deeply, yes. It altered my childhood, yes. It shaped my patterns of love and fear. But it did not destroy me. Even shattered glass can reflect light. Even broken trust can, in time, be pieced together with care, with gentleness, with healing.

At the time, I could not see that possibility. I only felt the fracture the deep ache of being unable to trust the world I lived in. My heart, once open, curled into itself for protection. My soul, once eager to believe, wrapped itself in caution. I was a child learning a lesson no child should ever have to learn: that sometimes the ones who smile at you, feed you, even tuck you into bed, are the very ones who can hurt you most.

That was the wound of shattered trust. And it followed me, like a shadow, through every doorway, every friendship, every relationship that came after. But it also became the starting place of my eventual strength the moment I stopped depending on others to keep me safe, and began to long for the day I would learn to keep myself safe.

Chapter 8 – Silent Cries

Not every cry for help is loud. Not every scream tears through the air. Sometimes, the deepest cries are silent, hidden beneath forced smiles, muffled by fear, or buried under a mask of strength. Those were my cries the cries no one heard, the ones I barely allowed myself to acknowledge.

As a child, I wanted desperately for someone to see me, to notice the truth I could not speak aloud. I wanted an adult to look past my surface and recognize the shadows lurking in my eyes. I wanted a teacher to pause long enough to sense that my quietness was not shyness but sorrow. I wanted a friend to notice that my laughter sometimes broke too quickly, that my silences were too heavy for someone so young.

But my cries were silent, and silence is easy to ignore.

I remember sitting in classrooms, my books open, my hands folded neatly, while my mind screamed for rescue. I remember lying awake at night, staring at the ceiling, hoping someone would come through the door and tell me it was over. I remember the ache in my chest when I tried to speak, when the words nearly slipped out, only to retreat back into my throat, swallowed whole by fear.

These were not cries that could be measured in sound. They were seen only in the subtle ways a child changes under the weight of pain. The way my shoulders curled inward, as if to protect myself from a world too harsh. The way my eyes avoided contact, afraid that someone might see too much. The way my laughter felt thin, hollow, and fleeting, like a candle flame flickering in the wind.

Children are often expected to be resilient, adaptable, unbreakable in their innocence. But the truth is, children do cry out they just don't always use words. Their cries are written in their behavior, in their silence, in their restlessness, in their withdrawal. I cried out in every way I could, except with my voice. And still, no one heard. Or perhaps, no one wanted to.

There is a particular loneliness in crying silently. It convinces you that you are invisible, that your pain does not matter, that even if you tried to speak, it would only echo back into emptiness. Silent cries are swallowed by the walls of bedrooms, absorbed by the air of classrooms, dismissed by the busyness of adults who do not look closely enough. And so, I kept crying in silence, year after year, until it became second nature.

Looking back, I sometimes wonder how different things might have been if just one person had paused long enough to notice. If just one adult had asked the right question, looked me in the eyes, and waited patiently for the answer. Maybe I would have found the courage to whisper the truth. Maybe the silence would have cracked sooner. Maybe the cries would not have remained unheard for so long.

But I also know this: my silent cries were not wasted. Even though the world did not hear them, even though no one listened in that moment, they were a form of resistance. They were proof that I still longed for freedom, proof that I still believed, somewhere deep inside, that rescue was possible. Silent though they were, they carried my hope. And hope, even in silence, is powerful.

Now, as I write these words, my silent cries transform into sound, into story, into truth. They no longer hide in the dark corners of my memory; they take shape on the page, where they cannot be ignored. What was once silent now speaks. What was once unseen now demands to be recognized.

This chapter is for every child whose cries are muffled by fear, disbelief, or neglect. You are not unheard. You are not invisible. Your silence is not emptiness it is the sound of survival. And one day, like me, you may find your voice rising from that silence, strong and undeniable.

Chapter 9 – Promises and Predators

Predators rarely arrive with fangs bared or cruelty on display. They come cloaked in charm, in trustworthiness, in the comforting disguise of safety. They carry words that sound like kindness, gestures that mimic care, and promises that shimmer like hope to a child longing to be loved. That is how predators move quietly, strategically, blending into the ordinary until their true intentions surface.

I was only a child, hungry for affection, desperate for someone to see me, to affirm me, to make me feel wanted. And predators sense that hunger the way wolves smell blood. They know what words to use, what smiles to offer, what promises to make. You are special. This is just between us. I'll always protect you. Promises like those became the soft chains around my wrists, invisible but unbreakable.

The promises were not grand, not glittering. They were simple sometimes as small as a gift, a secret, or a kind word. But to a child, they meant everything. They made me believe I had a bond, a connection, something worth holding onto. Yet each promise was a lie, designed not to give but to take. Designed to keep me quiet, to keep me obedient, to keep me tethered to someone who saw me not as a child but as prey.

That is the hardest truth to face that predators do not only use force. They use affection. They use familiarity. They use the very language of love to ensnare those too young to distinguish genuine care from calculated deceit. And so, I fell into their web, not because I was weak, but because I was human. Because I was a child who wanted to believe in love, in safety, in promises kept.

But every promise carried a shadow. I'll keep you safe meant as long as you stay silent. You are special meant you belong to me, not to yourself. This is our secret meant you must carry my guilt on your small shoulders. What felt like care was control. What looked like affection was manipulation. What sounded like love was abuse.

And predators thrive in the silence those promises create. They rely on a child's inability to discern the difference between truth and deception, between love and exploitation. They rely on the world's refusal to question, on society's habit of looking away. And they rely on the broken trust of a child who no longer knows what safety feels like.

I carried those promises like curses. Each one etched itself into me, convincing me that I was trapped, that I could not leave, that no one else would ever want me. That is the other cruelty of predators: they do not only harm you in the moment they rewrite the way you see yourself. They make you believe you are powerless, voiceless, invisible.

And yet, deep inside, a small part of me resisted. Even as I repeated their promises in my head, even as I clung to the illusion that they might mean something good, there was a voice whispering: This is wrong. This is not love. This is not care. That whisper was faint, often drowned out by fear and shame, but it kept me from completely surrendering to the lies.

Looking back, I see now that predators build their power not on their strength but on the silence of their victims. Their promises are tools of manipulation, designed to shield themselves and isolate the child. And yet, when the silence is broken, those promises lose their grip. When the lies are named, the predator is unmasked.

This chapter is not only about the predators who took advantage of me. It is about the countless children around the world whose innocence is stolen through false promises. It is about the predators who still walk freely, hiding behind masks of respectability, cloaked in the trust of their communities. And it is about the importance of seeing through the promises, of teaching children and adults alike that love does not demand secrets, that protection does not come with conditions, that promises made in darkness are not promises at all.

The predators thought their promises would silence me forever. But here, in these pages, I shatter them. I name them for what they were: lies. And in doing so, I reclaim the truth that was stolen from me that I was worthy of love, of protection, of safety, without conditions, without chains, without predators.

Chapter 10 – Living in the Shadows

To live in the shadows is to exist without fully being seen. It is to walk through the world like a ghost present, breathing, moving but never truly alive in the light. That was my life for years, a quiet existence in which my laughter was borrowed, my words were cautious, and my steps were measured. On the surface, I looked like any other girl, but beneath the surface, I was someone else entirely someone marked by fear, someone carrying a story too heavy for her small frame.

The shadows became my hiding place. They were both my refuge and my prison. In the shadows, I could pretend that nothing had happened. I could blend in, unnoticed, as though invisibility might protect me. Yet the same shadows also smothered me, suffocating me with secrets I could not share, pressing me down with silence I could not break.

There is a peculiar way abuse forces you into duality. You become two people at once. By day, I was the obedient daughter, the quiet student, the polite child who smiled when expected. By night or behind closed doors I was the frightened, voiceless version of myself, carrying wounds I could not name. That split life felt like walking in shadows, never fully one thing, never fully the other, always trapped in-between.

The shadows shaped everything. They dictated how I spoke, how I sat, how I interacted with others. I learned to avoid drawing attention to myself, fearing that too much light might expose me. I smiled at the right moments, kept my head low, and laughed when others laughed, though my heart was heavy. I mastered the art of pretending, of fading into the background, of ensuring no one looked too closely.

But living in the shadows comes at a cost. Over time, the shadows seep inside you, convincing you that invisibility is safer than being seen, that silence is safer than speaking, that numbness is easier than feeling. You begin to lose sight of who you are beyond the shadows, until one day you wake up and realize you no longer know yourself at all.

Still, there was a part of me small, fragile, but alive that longed for the light. Sometimes it revealed itself in the simplest ways: the way I tilted my face toward the sun, as if soaking in warmth I wasn't sure I deserved; the way I wrote words in secret journals, hoping they might one day set me free; the way I looked at others, wishing I could be as carefree, as unburdened, as whole as they seemed to be. Those moments were flickers of light in the darkness, proof that even in the shadows, hope stubbornly survives.

Yet for years, I stayed there, in that half-life. Living in the shadows became second nature. I convinced myself it was safer to be unseen, to keep my story hidden, to let the world believe its comfortable illusions. But deep inside, I knew shadows could never sustain me. Sooner or later, I would have to step out, to confront what was done to me, to name it, to drag it into the light where it could no longer control me.

Living in the shadows was my survival, but it was not my destiny. The shadows carried me through the darkest times, but they were never meant to hold me forever. And though it would take years, though it would take courage I didn't yet know I had, I would eventually find my way out. I would learn that there is life beyond the shadows and that my story, no matter how painful, deserved the light.

PART 3 - THE COURAGE TO SPEAK

For so long, my voice was a prisoner. It lived behind locked lips, buried beneath layers of fear, shame, and uncertainty. Every time I tried to speak, the words felt too heavy, too dangerous, as though saying them aloud would shatter me or make the world collapse. Silence had become my shield, my way of surviving but silence also chained me to my pain.

Finding the courage to speak did not happen all at once. It was not a dramatic outburst, not a sudden flood of words after years of keeping them in. It began as a whisper inside me, faint but persistent, urging me toward freedom. That whisper grew louder each time I felt the weight of my secrets pressing too hard on my chest, each time I realized that silence was protecting the wrong people the predators, the abusers while suffocating the innocent me.

Speaking felt like standing at the edge of a cliff, unsure whether I would fall or finally learn to fly. I feared no one would believe me. I feared I would be blamed, shamed, or punished. I feared that the moment the words left my mouth, I would no longer be able to control the story. That is the cruel trick of trauma it convinces you that your silence is the only thing keeping you safe, when in truth, it is the silence that keeps you trapped.

But somewhere deep within, I realized that if I didn't speak, I would disappear entirely. My story would be swallowed, my pain ignored, my life reduced to shadows. And so, trembling, with my heart pounding so hard I thought it would burst, I let the words begin to form. At first, they were clumsy, broken, fragments of a truth I struggled to hold. But once spoken, they carried a power I had never known.

The first time I told my story, it did not feel like relief it felt like terror. My voice shook, my hands trembled, and I wanted desperately to take the words back, to stuff them inside me again. But with each word that passed my lips, something shifted. I was reclaiming myself, piece by piece. My voice, once stolen, was becoming mine again.

Courage is not the absence of fear it is moving forward despite fear. And that is what speaking was for me. I was terrified, but I spoke anyway. I was uncertain, but I spoke anyway. I was fragile, but I spoke anyway. Because I knew, finally, that my silence had protected my abusers long enough. My voice belonged to me, and it was time to use it.

In speaking, I discovered something unexpected: I was not alone. My words reached others who had lived in silence too, others who carried their own shadows and secrets. And in their eyes, I saw recognition, solidarity, and strength. That realization was more healing than I could have imagined that my story, once a source of shame, could become a source of connection and even empowerment.

The courage to speak does not erase the pain. It does not make the memories vanish or undo the harm. But it does something almost as powerful: it breaks the hold of silence. It strips predators of their greatest weapon secrecy. And it allows healing to begin, however slowly, however unevenly.

Now, as I write these words, I think of the child I once was the girl of nobody, who cried silently in the dark, who lived in the shadows, who believed her voice did not matter. To her, I say: we found the courage. We spoke. And in speaking, we began to heal.

This chapter is for every survivor standing on the edge of that cliff, wondering if they have the strength to let the words come out. You do. Your voice is powerful. Your story matters. And no matter how broken you may feel, the moment you speak, you step into your power.

Speaking was not the end of my journey it was the beginning.

Chapter 11 – Finding My Voice

For years, my voice was something I could not find. It hid in corners, trembling, too fragile to face the world. Even when I spoke, it was never truly mine it was shaped by fear, hushed by shame, bent by the expectations of others. But slowly, after daring to speak my truth for the first time, something within me began to shift. The silence I had carried for so long started to crack, and in those cracks, I began to hear myself more clearly.

Finding my voice was not a single moment of triumph. It was a journey, full of stumbles and second-guessing, moments where I almost retreated back into silence. But with every word I dared to speak, my voice grew stronger. It was like learning to walk all over again awkward at first, but each step leading me further away from the shadows that had once defined me.

My voice began to show itself in unexpected ways. In journals filled with unfiltered thoughts. In small conversations where I finally admitted what had happened to me. In the way I carried myself my back a little straighter, my eyes a little steadier. Each act of expression, no matter how small, was a declaration that I was still here, still alive, still mine.

And with that voice came something I never thought I would feel: power. Not the kind of power that controls or dominates, but the kind of power that restores. The power of saying this happened to me without shame. The power of refusing to carry someone else's guilt. The power of rewriting my story in my own words, instead of living by the lies of others.

For so long, predators had used my silence as their weapon. They thrived in it, hid behind it, depended on it. But when I found my voice, that weapon broke. I realized that speaking my truth was not only an act of survival it was an act of defiance. Every word I spoke tore down the walls that had trapped me, brick by brick.

Finding my voice also meant finding myself. Beneath the pain and the secrets, there was still a girl who loved to laugh, who dreamed of a future brighter than her past, who longed to be free. My voice helped me connect with her again, to remind myself that I was more than what was done to me. I was not only a survivor of pain—I was a bearer of truth.

And truth is liberating. It does not erase the scars, but it transforms them. It turns wounds into testimonies, silence into strength, shame into resilience. My voice carried not just my story but the promise that I was no longer bound by what happened in the dark. I was stepping into the light, word by word, sentence by sentence.

Now, when I think of the frightened child who once believed she had no voice, I feel a tenderness for her. She did not know then that her silence would one day give way to a voice strong enough to tell her story. She did not know that her whispers would grow into a song of survival. She did not know that her voice, once hidden, would one day rise not just for herself, but for others still living in the shadows.

Finding my voice was not the end of my journey, but it was the foundation of everything that followed. It gave me the courage to face the world as I was broken, healing, growing and to believe that my story could matter.

Because once you find your voice, you can never truly lose it again. It becomes your anchor, your compass, your freedom.

Chapter 12– When No One Believed Me

Speaking was supposed to bring relief. I thought that once the words left my lips, the weight of silence would finally be lifted, that someone would hold me close, believe me, and promise that I was safe now. But instead of comfort, I was met with doubt. Instead of protection, I was met with questions, suspicion, and silence that cut even deeper than the one I had broken.

The first time I told the truth, I expected the world to shift. I thought people would rush in, horrified, ready to shield me from further harm. Instead, their faces hardened, their eyes narrowed, and their words pierced sharper than any blade: Are you sure? Maybe you misunderstood. You must be exaggerating. Don't ruin a family's reputation over this.

Each word was a dismissal, a denial of my pain, a rewriting of my truth before it even had a chance to breathe. I had been brave enough to speak, but my bravery was met not with validation, but with disbelief. And disbelief is its own kind of betrayal.

To not be believed after finding the courage to speak is like being silenced all over again but louder, harsher, crueler. It teaches you that your voice is dangerous, that your truth is unwanted, that your pain is too inconvenient for others to acknowledge. It crushes the fragile hope that maybe, just maybe, you were not alone in this.

I remember feeling smaller than ever, shrinking back into myself, ashamed not only of what had happened to me but now of daring to say it aloud. The world seemed to tell me: better to keep quiet, better to bury it, better to forget. But forgetting was impossible. And burying the truth only made it burn hotter inside me.

What hurt most was not only the disbelief, but who it came from. Sometimes it was adults I had trusted, people who should have been my protectors. Sometimes it was peers, who laughed it off or turned away. And sometimes, it was the silence of those who heard and said nothing at all that heavy silence that spoke louder than words: We don't want to deal with this. We'd rather you stay quiet.

The predators' greatest weapon had always been my silence, but disbelief gave them something even more powerful: protection. When others chose not to believe me, they shielded the very people who had harmed me. They made me carry not only the weight of my trauma but also the weight of their denial.

And yet, even in the sting of disbelief, I learned something important: my truth did not become less true because others refused to accept it. Their denial did not erase what happened. Their silence did not undo my pain. My story belonged to me, and it was real, whether or not the world wanted to face it.

That realization did not erase the hurt of not being believed, but it planted a seed of resilience. If others would not stand for me, then I would learn, slowly and painfully, to stand for myself. If others tried to silence me, then I would learn to speak louder. If others doubted me, then I would learn to stop needing their approval to validate my reality.

Being disbelieved nearly broke me, but in time, it also forged a strength I didn't know I had. It taught me to cling to my own truth, to honor my own voice, to know that surviving was not dependent on others' recognition, but on my own courage to keep going.

This chapter is for every survivor who dared to speak and was met with disbelief. You are not alone. Your truth is still truth, even if the world turns its back on it. And though disbelief wounds deeply, it cannot erase what happened. It cannot silence what is real.

In the end, I learned that belief from others is powerful, but belief in yourself belief in your own story, your own worth, your own voice is unshakable. And once I held onto that, no one's disbelief could ever take it away again.

Chapter 13 – The Power of Telling the Truth

For so long, the truth felt like a dangerous thing. I kept it hidden, convinced that if I ever let it out, it would destroy me. The lies of my abusers were easier for the world to accept than the reality of my pain, and so I swallowed the truth, carrying it quietly like a secret poison inside me. But secrets rot the soul. They weigh you down until you can barely breathe. And there comes a moment when holding the truth inside becomes more unbearable than the risk of letting it out.

When I finally began to speak the truth, I did not yet understand its power. At first, it felt raw, terrifying like peeling back layers of my skin and exposing wounds I had tried so hard to hide. But as the words left me, I realized something I had never felt before: freedom. My truth was no longer locked inside me; it was alive, out in the open, no longer shackled to my silence.

There is power in truth because it cannot be changed by denial. Others may doubt it, dismiss it, or try to twist it, but the truth itself remains unshaken. For every time someone tried to silence me, the truth kept rising, like a current too strong to be dammed. It carried me forward, even when I stumbled, even when fear whispered that it would be safer to go back into hiding.

Telling the truth broke the chains my abusers had wrapped around me. They had thrived on my silence, building their control on the foundation of secrets. By speaking, I shattered that foundation. I took away their power to define me, to own my story. With every retelling, with every step into the light, I reclaimed another piece of myself.

But the power of truth went beyond me. I saw how it reached others, survivors who heard my words and recognized their own hidden scars. Truth creates connection. It strips away the illusion of isolation, reminding us that we are not alone in our pain. And in that connection, healing begins not just for me, but for all of us who have carried our silence for too long.

There is also a justice in truth. Even when systems fail, even when the world turns a blind eye, truth itself is a form of justice. It names what was done. It calls out what was wrong. It refuses to let cruelty stay hidden. Truth exposes. And in exposing, it begins to dismantle the power of those who harm.

I learned that telling the truth is not only about the past it is about the future. It is about building a life where silence no longer defines me, where shame no longer rules me, where fear no longer cages me. It is about creating a path for the child I once was, and for the countless others still trapped in silence, to believe that their voices matter too.

The truth is not easy. It is not painless. But it is powerful. It is the torch that lights the way out of the shadows. It is the anchor that keeps me steady when disbelief tries to shake me. It is the weapon that dismantles lies and restores dignity.

Telling my truth did not erase what happened, but it transformed me. It turned my pain into purpose, my silence into strength, my past into testimony. And in speaking it, I became something I had never believed I could be: free.

This chapter is for every survivor holding a truth too heavy to carry alone. Know this: your truth is not your burden it is your power. And when you are ready to speak it, it will set you free.

PART 4 - JUSTICE AND RESISTANCE

Justice is a word that once felt unreachable to me. For so long, I thought justice meant punishment handed down by courts, apologies that never came, or a restoration of the innocence I had lost. And because none of that came quickly because sometimes it never comes at all I believed justice was something forever denied to me. But with time, I began to see that justice is not only what the world gives you it is also what you claim for yourself.

The first form of justice I found was survival itself. To live, to breathe, to keep moving despite what was done to me that was resistance. My abusers thrived on my silence, but each day I woke up and refused to let their actions define me was an act of rebellion. Survival was my protest, my quiet declaration that they had not won.

Still, survival was not enough. I longed for accountability for the truth to be known, for those who harmed me to face the consequences of their choices. But justice is not simple for survivors. The systems we are told to trust often fail us. People look away, evidence is dismissed, and predators are protected by silence, power, or denial. There were times when it felt like justice was a mirage something I could see in the distance but never touch.

Yet resistance taught me another truth: even when the world refuses to hold predators accountable, there are still ways to reclaim justice. Speaking out was justice. Naming what was done to me was justice. Refusing to carry their shame was justice. Each step I took to rebuild my life, each choice I made to live without apology, was justice.

Resistance is not always loud. Sometimes it is quiet, steady, relentless. It is the decision to heal even when wounds still ache. It is the choice to believe in your worth even when others deny it. It is the power to stand tall, to refuse to shrink, to refuse to disappear. Resistance is taking back what trauma tried to steal—my voice, my freedom, my future.

But resistance also grew beyond me. I realized that my story was not only my own; it was part of a larger struggle, a shared fight for every child silenced, every survivor dismissed, every voice pushed into the shadows. Speaking my truth was no longer just for me it was for the girls and boys who had not yet found their voices, for the ones still trapped in silence, for the ones who feared that no one would ever believe them.

Justice, then, became more than punishment. It became transformation. It became creating spaces where silence could not rule, where predators could not hide, where survivors could be heard and believed. And resistance became the lifeline that carried me forward the determination to live fully, to love myself fiercely, to turn my pain into purpose.

To this day, I know the scales of justice may never balance perfectly. There are wounds that cannot be erased, years that cannot be returned, scars that will never fade. But I have found my own form of justice in truth, in survival, in resilience, and in resistance. I carry it with me like armor, not to erase my past, but to remind myself that I am more powerful than what tried to destroy me.

This chapter is for every survivor still searching for justice, for everyone who feels the weight of systems that fail them, for every soul who wonders if resistance is enough. Know this: your survival is resistance. Your voice is justice. Your very existence, after everything you've endured, is proof that you are unbreakable.

And sometimes, that is the greatest justice of all.

Chapter 14 – Into the Courts

The courtroom was supposed to be a place of justice, but to me, it felt like another battlefield. Walking into those walls, I carried not only my story but also the heavy burden of proving it of laying bare my deepest wounds before strangers who would measure, question, and dissect them.

The air inside the courtroom was thick, sterile, unforgiving. Everything about it was designed for order wooden benches, polished floors, the raised desk where the judge sat, elevated above everyone else. But to me, it did not feel like order. It felt like exposure. Every eye seemed to pierce through me, demanding answers, demanding composure, demanding a strength I wasn't sure I had.

I had always believed that the hardest part was surviving the abuse itself. I never imagined that telling the truth in front of the law would feel like reliving it all over again. Every question pulled me backward, back into the darkness I was trying to escape. Every detail I was forced to recount felt like reopening wounds that had barely begun to heal.

And worse than the questions were the doubts. Lawyers, with their sharp words and sharpened faces, twisted my story as if it were nothing more than a puzzle to be solved, a performance to be picked apart. They asked in ways that made me question myself: Are you sure? Could you be mistaken? Why didn't you tell sooner? Each question was not just an inquiry but an accusation, dressed in the language of law.

The courts, I learned, are not built for children, nor for survivors. They are built for evidence, for procedure, for the weighing of facts against doubt. But trauma does not fit neatly into legal language. Memories blur, timelines tangle, emotions overwhelm. And yet, there I was, expected to make my pain palatable, to deliver my story in a way that could be measured, dissected, and stamped "credible."

It was exhausting, humiliating, and at times, crushing. I wanted to scream: Why must I fight so hard to prove what was done to me? Why am I the one on trial, when it was me who was harmed?

And yet, I also found within myself a strength I didn't know was there. Each time I spoke, despite the tremor in my voice, I was reclaiming my power. Each time I stood in that courtroom, I was defying the silence that predators had forced upon me. No matter how cold the system felt, no matter how bruising the process was, I reminded myself: I belong here. My truth belongs here.

The courts did not give me the kind of justice I once dreamed of. They did not erase the past or undo the harm. But walking into that room, standing before judges and lawyers, speaking the words I had once been too afraid to whisper that, in itself, was a form of justice. It was me saying: I will no longer be silent. I will not disappear. You cannot erase me.

What I learned is that justice is not always a verdict. Sometimes, it is the act of standing tall in spaces meant to intimidate you. Sometimes, it is refusing to be broken, even when the system feels indifferent to your pain. Sometimes, it is simply showing up, with your truth intact, and speaking anyway.

This chapter is for every survivor who has walked into a courtroom carrying the weight of their story. Whether you were believed or dismissed, whether justice was served or denied, know this: the very act of entering that space and refusing silence is powerful. You were brave. You were unshakable. And no verdict, no gavel, no system can take that away.

Chapter 15– The Shield of Power

Power protects. Not always the vulnerable, not always the broken, but too often the ones who harm. I learned this bitter truth when I began to understand how deeply the people who abused me, and those who enabled them, were shielded not by innocence, but by the armor of power.

The shield of power does not always look obvious. Sometimes it is money, capable of buying silence, swaying lawyers, or stretching trials until survivors are exhausted into surrender. Sometimes it is reputation, a carefully built façade that convinces the world that a person could never be guilty of the horrors whispered against them. And sometimes it is simply silence—friends, families, or institutions choosing to look the other way, protecting the abuser rather than the child.

I watched as power cloaked those who hurt me. People who should have been held accountable were instead defended, excused, or ignored. Their words were believed more than mine, not because of truth, but because of their standing, their influence, or their ability to intimidate. It was like screaming into the wind, my voice swept away by the storm of their authority.

What hurt the most was not only what was done to me, but how others protected those who did it. Some did it knowingly, choosing comfort over confrontation. Others did it quietly, convincing themselves it was "not their place" to intervene. And then there were those who benefited from the power, clinging to its shadow because it gave them safety, security, or status. In their silence, I was betrayed again and again.

The shield of power is a cruel weapon because it forces survivors into invisibility. It makes us doubt ourselves. It whispers: No one will believe you. They are too strong, too respected, too untouchable. And for a long time, I believed that. For a long time, I let the weight of their power convince me that my voice was too small to matter.

But power is not always what it seems. It is fragile, held together by lies and silence. And once the truth begins to break through, cracks form in even the strongest shield. That realization became a turning point for me. I began to see that my words, my story, my survival, were weapons too. They were not backed by wealth or influence, but they were sharpened by truth.

I will not pretend that breaking through the shield of power was easy. It wasn't. It meant losing people I thought would stand by me. It meant being called names, being doubted, being accused of destroying reputations that, in truth, had destroyed themselves. It meant facing isolation and rejection. But it also meant freedom. Because once I stopped fearing their power, I realized they had less of it than they wanted me to believe.

The shield of power protects predators, but it also imprisons them. They live in fear of exposure, in constant need to maintain their false image, to silence every whisper. My freedom came in knowing that while they had power in the world's eyes, I had truth in mine. And truth, even when doubted, even when buried, never dies.

This chapter is not only about the shield that covered them it is about the courage it took to step out from under its shadow. To every survivor who has felt silenced by someone else's power, know this: power does not make them invincible. Their shield is not impenetrable. And your voice, though it may tremble, has the strength to pierce through it.

Because in the end, no shield no matter how polished, no matter how strong can stand forever against the weight of truth.

Chapter 16 – Small Victories, Heavy Losses

People like to believe that justice arrives neatly wrapped, that once the truth is spoken and the system hears it, everything falls into place. They imagine survivors walking away whole, smiling, healed, with the past neatly folded behind them. But that is not how it happens. Justice if it comes at all often comes in fragments. Small victories, fleeting and fragile. And those victories rarely arrive without heavy losses trailing behind them.

I remember the first moment I felt a spark of victory. It was not when a judge spoke or when lawyers filed their papers. It was when I said my story aloud, in a place where silence had once been forced upon me. For the first time, I felt the weight of my own courage. That was a victory small, invisible to anyone else, but monumental to me.

Later, when whispers turned to acknowledgments, when people who once doubted me began to say, I believe you, that too felt like a victory. But even then, it was complicated. Because those words did not erase the years of disbelief. They did not heal the scars left by silence. They were like drops of water after a long drought welcome, life-giving, but never enough to undo the dryness that had already cracked the earth.

Some victories came in the form of accountability, though rarely the kind I longed for. A predator exposed, a reputation stained, a door of silence forced open. But even in those moments, the losses lingered. Relationships fractured. Communities divided. People I loved chose sides, and too often, they chose comfort over truth. To stand for myself meant standing apart, and that loneliness was a loss that shadowed every step forward.

The heaviest losses, though, were internal. No courtroom, no acknowledgment, no whispered apology could give me back my childhood. No system could restore the trust that had been shattered, or erase the nights I lay awake, carrying fear like a second skin. Those were losses permanent, woven into the fabric of who I was becoming. They are scars I will always carry, even alongside the victories.

Yet, I learned something important: small victories matter. They may not erase the pain, but they carve out spaces of hope. They are proof that silence does not always win, that lies do not last forever, that predators are not untouchable. Each victory, no matter how small, was a stepping stone toward reclaiming my life.

But I refuse to romanticize them. Survivors should not have to trade pieces of their lives just to be believed. We should not have to lose family, community, or peace of mind to gain recognition of the truth. And yet, that is the reality we are too often forced to live with one where victories are stitched together with grief.

Still, I hold onto those victories, because they remind me of something larger: that even in the midst of losses, I endured. That even when the system gave me scraps of justice instead of wholeness, I kept moving. That even when the cost was high, I refused to disappear.

Small victories may not heal everything, but they are proof of survival. And survival, in a world that tried to erase me, is the greatest triumph of all.

Chapter 17 – Standing Against Giants

For so long, my fight had been against individuals the ones who harmed me, the ones who silenced me, the ones who doubted me. But as I grew stronger, I began to see that what I was fighting was not only them. I was fighting something much larger: the giants that stand behind them. Giants made of silence, of culture, of power, of systems built to protect everything but the truth.

These giants are everywhere. They live in institutions that value reputation over justice. They thrive in families that whisper don't talk about it rather than confront the rot in their own homes. They sit inside courtrooms where procedure is worshipped more than humanity. They are strengthened by communities that prefer the illusion of peace over the disruption of truth.

Standing against these giants felt overwhelming. How could someone like me scarred, silenced, dismissed ever have the strength to challenge them? They towered above me, casting shadows that stretched across every corner of my life. And yet, I realized something: giants are not invincible. They may look larger than life, but they are built on fear, silence, and complicity. And once you stop being silent, once you stop being afraid, the giant begins to shrink.

It wasn't easy. Every step I took against these forces felt like walking into a storm. Speaking out meant more isolation, more whispers, more people turning their backs. But each time I spoke, I chipped away at the armor of those giants. Each time I refused to bow down to silence, I reminded myself: I am no longer small. I am no longer powerless.

There is courage in naming what others want hidden. There is resistance in refusing to protect the predators they shield. And there is freedom in standing up, even when your legs shake, even when your voice trembles. Because standing against giants is not about being fearless it is about standing despite the fear.

The truth is, giants feed on silence. That is their greatest strength. And when survivors speak when we rise, when we tell our stories, when we refuse to be erased we strip them of their power. That is how change begins. Not all at once, not with immediate victories, but with the steady, unyielding force of truth.

I have come to see that standing against giants is not just about me. It is about the children who will come after me, the survivors who are still silenced, the voices that are still trapped in the shadows. Every word I speak, every act of resistance, is for them too. Because one survivor speaking alone may seem small, but when we speak together, our voices become an earthquake, shaking the ground beneath those giants.

I do not pretend the fight is over. The giants still exist. They still tower in courts, in homes, in institutions, in cultures that dismiss survivors. But I have learned that they are not unshakable. And I have learned that my voice, though once stolen, is now a weapon strong enough to stand against them.

So I stand not because it is easy, not because I do not fear, but because I refuse to bow. And in that act of defiance, I have found a truth I once thought impossible: even the tallest giants can fall.

PART V - BECOMING WHOLE AGAIN

There comes a moment in every survivor's journey when the fight for justice, the struggle against silence, and the battles with giants leave you standing in a strange place alive, defiant, but still broken inside. For so long, my life had been consumed with surviving, with speaking out, with standing tall against everything that sought to erase me. But once the noise of those battles began to quiet, I was left with something far more intimate, far more difficult: the work of healing myself.

Becoming whole again is not about erasing the past. It is not about pretending the abuse never happened or burying the scars so deep that no one can see them. Wholeness is not forgetting it is integrating. It is learning how to live with the pieces of yourself that were once shattered and finding a way to arrange them into something new, something strong, something beautiful.

For a long time, I thought healing meant waiting for others to repair what they had broken. I waited for apologies that never came. I waited for justice that was incomplete. I waited for the world to look at me differently, to finally see the truth of my pain. But healing, I learned, does not wait for anyone else. Healing begins when we decide that our lives are too precious to leave in the hands of those who harmed us. Healing is a choice a slow, painful, courageous choice to reclaim what was stolen and to write the rest of our story in our own words.

This part of my journey was not about courts, not about systems, not about proving myself to anyone else. It was about turning inward. It was about sitting with my wounds, listening to them, and gently teaching myself that I was not defined by them. It was about daring to believe that I deserved love, peace, and joy, even after everything I had endured.

Becoming whole again does not mean being unscarred. It means wearing those scars as proof that you survived, as evidence of your resilience. It means transforming the silence into songs of strength, the fear into freedom, the pain into purpose. It means no longer carrying shame that was never mine to bear.

This is the chapter of rebirth. The part where brokenness is not the end of the story, but the soil where new life takes root. Where survival is no longer just about getting through the day, but about learning how to thrive. Where I begin to discover myself beyond the identity of "victim" or even "survivor" to discover myself as whole, as human, as worthy of everything beautiful that life still has to offer.

In the pages that follow, I share the slow, tender work of becoming whole again. The invisible wounds. The sisters of survival. The power of advocacy. The future that once felt impossible but is now mine to shape. This is not the end of the journey but it is a new beginning.

Because the truth is this: no matter what was taken, no matter what was broken, no matter how heavy the past may feel wholeness is still possible. And I am living proof.

Chapter 18 – Healing the Invisible Wounds

The world often looks at scars as proof of survival. They are visible, tangible, and undeniable. But the deepest wounds are not always on the skin they live inside, where no one else can see them. They are the nightmares that wake you in the middle of the night, the sudden flood of fear when you hear a certain voice, the shame that lingers in silence, even when you know it is not yours to carry. These invisible wounds are the hardest to explain, and they are the hardest to heal.

For years, I carried them quietly. To the outside world, I seemed fine walking, talking, functioning. But inside, I was bleeding. I had mastered the art of pretending, of smiling when expected, of nodding when people said, You're so strong. They never knew that strength often felt like a mask I wore so that no one could see how broken I still felt.

Healing these wounds was not as simple as time passing. People love to say, time heals all wounds, but that is not true. Time only buries them deeper unless you face them. And facing them is terrifying. It meant going back into the memories I had tried so hard to lock away. It meant sitting with the child I once was and listening to her cries, even when they shattered me. It meant naming what I had once refused to name, letting the pain come to the surface instead of burying it under silence.

Therapy helped. Writing helped. Speaking my truth helped. But healing was not a straight path it was a jagged, uneven journey. There were days when I felt like I had conquered the darkness, only to wake the next morning drowning in it again. Healing, I learned, is not about reaching a perfect state where the pain disappears. It is about learning to live with the scars in a way that does not control you anymore.

The hardest wound to heal was the shame. Shame is like poison it seeps into your soul, convincing you that the abuse was your fault, that you are dirty, that you will never be whole. It is a lie, but it is a lie that feels heavy and real. For a long time, I carried it as though it belonged to me. Only when I began to release that shame, to give it back to the ones who deserved it, did I begin to breathe again. That moment the quiet decision to say this was never my fault was the beginning of true healing.

Another invisible wound was trust. Trusting others felt impossible. How could I open my heart when it had been so brutally betrayed? But slowly, with patience and care, I learned that not everyone was a threat. I learned that there were people who could hold my story without judgment, who could sit with my pain without turning away. Trusting again did not happen overnight, but every time I let someone in, every time I allowed myself to believe in goodness again, the wound of betrayal began to close.

And then there was the wound of self-worth. Abuse had stripped me of the belief that I was valuable, lovable, or deserving of joy. Healing that wound required looking at myself with new eyes not through the lens of what had been done to me, but through the truth of who I was. It meant practicing self-love in small ways: resting when I was tired, saying no when I needed boundaries, speaking kindly to myself when old voices of self-hate tried to creep in.

Healing the invisible wounds will always be ongoing. There are days they ache more than others. There are moments when a sound, a smell, or a memory reopens them, and I am reminded that recovery is not a destination but a lifelong journey. But I have also discovered something beautiful: wounds can become wisdom. Pain can become power. And scars though invisible can still be proof of survival, proof of resilience, proof that I am still here.

This chapter is for every survivor who feels unseen because their wounds cannot be touched or traced. Your pain is real, even if the world cannot see it. Your healing is possible, even if it takes time. And your story though scarred is still sacred, still worthy, still whole.

Because healing is not about erasing what happened. It is about learning to live again not as the girl who was broken, but as the woman who survived.

Chapter 19 – Sisters of Survival

For much of my journey, I believed I was alone. Abuse isolates you it convinces you that no one else could possibly understand, that your pain is unique, your silence necessary, your shame inescapable. But when I began to hear the voices of others, women and girls whose stories echoed my own, I realized something life-changing: I was never truly alone. And neither were they.

Meeting other survivors was like finding pieces of myself I didn't know were missing. Their stories were not identical to mine every journey is different but the patterns of pain, silence, betrayal, and resilience wove our lives together like threads in the same tapestry. Listening to them was like listening to my own heart speak out loud, validating feelings I had once thought were too heavy, too strange, too unworthy to be named.

We became sisters not by blood, but by survival. And in that bond, I found healing I could never have reached on my own.

There is a sacred power in shared stories. When I spoke my truth to other survivors, there was no judgment, no disbelief, no sharp questions meant to pick apart my pain. There was only understanding. Nods. Tears. A quiet me too. In their eyes, I was not broken. I was not weak. I was not to blame. I was simply human, and I was believed.

With them, I could put down the mask. I did not have to pretend to be strong when I was tired, or smile when I wanted to cry. They knew the weight of invisible wounds, the way memories can hijack an ordinary day, the courage it takes just to keep living. In their presence, I could finally breathe freely.

But our bond was not only about shared pain it was also about shared strength. We reminded one another that survival is not shameful, it is heroic. We celebrated each other's victories, no matter how small: a day without nightmares, the courage to set boundaries, the act of telling our stories out loud. Every triumph, no matter how fragile, became proof that we were not just survivors we were warriors.

Sisters of survival also taught me that healing is not a solitary path. We are mirrors for one another, reflecting back the truth when we forget it ourselves. On the days I doubted my worth, they reminded me that I mattered. On the days I felt powerless, they reminded me of the battles I had already won. On the days I felt voiceless, they reminded me that my voice carried weight.

And beyond healing, we began to dream together. We imagined a world where girls like us would not have to fight so hard to be believed. We imagined systems that protected the vulnerable instead of shielding the powerful. We imagined raising our voices, not only for ourselves but for every child still trapped in silence. Together, we were no longer just survivors we were advocates, fighters, revolutionaries in our own right.

Sisters of survival are the family I chose, the community I never knew I needed. They are proof that pain can connect us, but so can hope. That trauma may have broken us apart, but love and solidarity can stitch us back together.

If there is one truth I want every survivor to know, it is this: you are not alone. There are others who understand, who believe you, who will walk beside you when the journey feels unbearable. Your story matters, your healing matters, and your survival is not just your own it is part of a greater strength that binds us all.

We are sisters. We are survivors. And together, we are unstoppable.

Chapter 20 – From Silence to Advocacy

For so many years, silence was my survival. I stayed quiet because I feared the consequences of speaking. I stayed quiet because I believed no one would listen, or worse, that no one would care. Silence was the armor I wore to protect myself in a world that preferred my pain hidden.

But silence, I came to learn, is not protection it is a prison. It shields predators, not survivors. It buries truth, not wounds. And in the quiet, shame grows heavier, deeper, stronger. The day I began to break that silence was the day I began to break free.

At first, my voice shook. I whispered my story in safe corners, to people I trusted, testing the waters of belief. And with each word, I felt something shift inside me. The shame I carried began to lift. The weight of secrecy began to crumble. It was terrifying, yes, but it was also liberating. Every time I spoke, the silence lost its grip.

Eventually, I realized that my story was more than just mine. It was part of a collective story a pattern of abuse, silence, and survival that spanned far beyond me. And once I saw that truth, I could no longer remain quiet. Advocacy was not a choice I stumbled upon; it was a calling that rose from the ashes of my pain.

Advocacy meant standing in places I once avoided courtrooms, schools, community halls and speaking my truth not just for myself, but for others who were still voiceless. It meant holding up my story like a mirror, so that the world could no longer pretend not to see. It meant turning my scars into a language of change.

But advocacy also came with risks. Speaking out invited criticism, disbelief, even hostility. There were people who told me I was "too much," that I was dwelling on the past, that I was breaking families or communities by daring to tell the truth. Yet I learned something powerful: their discomfort was not my burden. My voice was not the problem their silence was.

Through advocacy, I discovered purpose. I began to connect with others who had endured what I endured. I saw the way their eyes lit up when they heard someone speak aloud what they had buried in silence for years. I felt the power of shared courage, the way one story could spark another, and another, until silence itself began to crack.

From silence to advocacy, I learned that healing is not only about reclaiming my own life it is also about creating space for others to reclaim theirs. Advocacy is not about being the loudest voice in the room; it is about using your voice, however fragile or trembling, to make sure others know they are not alone.

And so I speak. I write. I stand. Not because the pain has disappeared, but because I refuse to let it be wasted. My story is my weapon, my shield, my offering. It belongs not only to me, but to every girl, every boy, every survivor who has been told to stay silent.

I may have once been a girl of nobody, but in advocacy, I have become somebody for myself, for others, for a movement that refuses to bow to silence. And in that transformation, I have found a deeper kind of healing: the healing that comes not only from surviving, but from helping others survive too.

Chapter 21 – A Future Beyond "Nobody"

For most of my life, I lived under the shadow of being nobody. That label was not always spoken aloud, but it was felt in the silence of those who ignored me, in the dismissal of those who doubted me, and in the cruelty of those who exploited my vulnerability. Being nobody was a wound, a curse, a cage I carried with me everywhere.

But survival, healing, and truth-telling taught me something radical: I was never nobody. I was always somebody worthy, valuable, powerful. The world tried to strip that truth from me, but it could not erase what was written in my spirit.

A future beyond "nobody" is a future of reclamation. It is reclaiming my name, my story, my dignity. It is standing tall, not as a victim bound to the past, but as a woman who carries her scars like medals of survival. My wounds are not proof of weakness; they are proof of endurance.

This future also means freedom the kind of freedom that comes when shame no longer holds the steering wheel of my life. I no longer shrink to fit into silence, nor do I apologize for existing. My presence, my voice, my truth they belong here. And they matter.

Beyond "nobody" also lies possibility. I see a life where joy is not stolen by memory, where trust is no longer a battlefield, where love is not poisoned by fear. I see myself building dreams once denied to me: friendships rooted in honesty, relationships built on respect, work that reflects my passion, and a life shaped by choice, not by chains.

But most of all, a future beyond "nobody" is not only about me it is about every survivor who has been made to feel invisible. When I speak, I carry them with me. When I rise, I rise for us all. When I envision a future, I see it not as a lonely path but as a shared journey, where no one is left behind in silence or despair.

I know there will still be days when the past tries to whisper in my ear, when memories knock against my heart, when fear attempts to return. But I also know this: I am no longer that powerless child. I am no longer voiceless. I am no longer trapped. My tomorrow is not determined by what happened yesterday.

I am somebody.

I am whole.

I am free.

And this is only the beginning of the story I was always meant to live.

EPILOGUE – THE ECHO OF SURVIVAL

When I look back on the girl I once was the girl who carried too many secrets, who lived in fear, who believed she was nobody I want to reach out and hold her. I want to tell her that survival does not make her less, that silence is not her destiny, and that the pain she carries will one day become a source of strength.

This book is not only the story of my past, but the testimony of my survival. It is proof that even in the darkest shadows, there is always a flicker of light. That even when silence feels suffocating, the voice inside us longs to break free. And that no matter how broken we may feel, healing is always possible.

But more than my story, this is our story. It belongs to every survivor who has been made invisible, every child who has been silenced, every woman or man who has carried wounds the world refuses to see. We are bound not only by pain, but by resilience. Not only by trauma, but by the fire that refuses to die out within us.

If you are reading this and see yourself in these words, let this epilogue be a message to you: you are not alone. Your voice matters. Your survival is not a mark of shame it is a badge of courage. And even if the world has tried to name you nobody, know this: you are somebody. You are worthy. You are loved.

As I step forward into the future, I carry this truth with me: survival is not the end of the story. It is the beginning of a new one. One shaped not by silence or fear, but by freedom, advocacy, and the unshakable belief that every life has value.

The echo of survival is not just in the scars we carry it is in the lives we build, the voices we raise, and the hope we pass on to others.

And so I close this chapter of my life with gratitude, with strength, and with a promise: to never again live as "nobody," but to walk boldly, fully, unapologetically as somebody.

The story does not end here.

It begins anew.

Acknowledgments

Writing this book has been a journey of courage, memory, and healing. Though the story belongs to me, it could never have been written without the love, support, and belief of so many along the way.

First and foremost, I want to thank every survivor who has ever shared their story with me whether in whispered conversations, in support groups, in courtrooms, or through written words. Your courage lit the path when mine faltered. You reminded me that survival is not shameful, but powerful. You gave me the strength to believe that silence can be broken and that truth can be spoken. This book is as much yours as it is mine.

To my sisters of survival you know who you are. Thank you for standing beside me when the weight of memory felt unbearable, for listening without judgment, for crying and laughing with me through the storms of healing. Our bond has been proof that even in the aftermath of betrayal, trust and love can be rebuilt.

To the advocates, counselors, and therapists who walk alongside survivors every day thank you for holding space for pain, for reminding us that we are not broken, and for offering tools to rebuild when it feels impossible. Your work is not just a profession it is a lifeline.

To those who believed me when others did not: you gave me back pieces of myself I thought were lost forever. Belief is a powerful thing; it can heal more than it seems. Thank you for seeing me, hearing me, and refusing to let my voice go unheard.

To my readers thank you for opening your hearts to this story. By turning these pages, you have joined me in breaking the silence. I hope these words meet you with compassion, whether you are a survivor seeking solace, an ally wanting to understand, or simply someone walking this earth with empathy in your heart. May you carry this story forward, not as a tale of tragedy, but as a testimony of resilience and the power of truth.

And finally, to the girl I once was the girl of "nobody." Thank you for surviving long enough to become the woman writing these words. Thank you for holding on in the moments when it would have been easier to give up. You were always worthy, even when the world told you otherwise. This book is my gift to you, and my promise that you will never again be unseen.

With every word, I honor those who came before me, those who walk beside me, and those who will come after. Together, we are not nobodies we are somebodies. And together, our voices will change the world.

Note to the Reader

Dear Reader,

If you have journeyed with me through these pages, I want to pause here and thank you not only for your time, but for the space you've given to this story. Reading about pain, survival, and healing is not easy. It stirs emotions, memories, and questions that can sit heavily on the heart. If at any point this book touched something tender inside of you, please know this: you are not alone.

Perhaps you read this book as a survivor yourself. If so, I see you. I believe you. And I honor the courage it takes just to keep living, to keep breathing, to keep moving forward, even when the world has tried to silence or diminish you. Your story matters whether you choose to speak it aloud or keep it close to your heart. Survival itself is a victory, and you carry within you a strength you may not yet fully see.

Perhaps you read as someone who loves a survivor. If so, thank you for opening your heart to understanding. Know that your presence, your patience, and your willingness to listen can be more healing than any grand gesture. To believe, to sit beside, to refuse to turn away these are gifts beyond measure.

And perhaps you read simply as a human being wanting to know, to feel, to connect. If so, may this story remind you of the quiet battles so many fight in silence. May it inspire you to listen more deeply, to speak more kindly, and to use whatever power you hold to make this world safer for the most vulnerable among us.

This book is not the end of the conversation. It is an opening, an invitation, a reminder. Healing is ongoing. Advocacy is ongoing. The fight for justice and safety is ongoing. My hope is that these pages serve not only as testimony of what was, but also as a spark for what can be for you, for me, for us all.

If you are carrying heavy feelings after reading, please take care of yourself. Step away, breathe deeply, rest. Talk to someone you trust. Reach out to a friend, a counselor, or a support group. You do not have to hold it all alone. There is no shame in needing help; in fact, asking for support is one of the bravest acts of survival.

From the deepest part of my heart, thank you for reading Girls of Nobody. Thank you for bearing witness. Thank you for caring enough to walk through the shadows with me. May you leave these pages carrying not only the weight of what happened, but also the light of resilience, hope, and the knowledge that none of us are truly "nobody."

With love and strength,

SOPHIA J BERG

Made in the USA
Middletown, DE
03 November 2025